Power of Concentration and Focus

Improve Your Life NOW

Elia Friedenthal

Table of Contents

INTRODUCTION

What is concentration?

Concentration is the capability to direct one's focus according to one's will. It indicates control of the attention. It is the ability to focus the mind on one topic, object or idea, and at the same time leave out from the mind every other unconnected opinion, concepts, sensations, and also sensations.

It additionally indicates the capacity to do something at a time, as opposed to leaping from one subject to one more and also losing time, attention, and power.

Focus is a state, in which one's whole interest is immersed in something just, and also ignoring every little thing else. During concentration, the mind concentrates on the characteristics of attention, and also only one thought occupies the mind. The total energy of the brain ends up being focused on this thought.

The capacity to command the mind and control the attention is not usual and calls for training. The majority of people do not have the ability to manage their focus and concentrate the mind specifically on one topic for any type of length of time. They can not command their mind to focus, whenever they want to. Concentration is not an unusual task. It occurs practically on a daily basis, to almost everybody. However, it is even more of a spontaneous and unrestrained capacity.

Have you seen just how young people don't hear you when they play? They wind up getting totally caught up in their computer game, unaware of everything else in all intents and purposes. At the point when you read a book that is amazingly entrancing, you don't hear individuals yelling or calling your name. You become unmindful of your surroundings, and lose any kind of sentiment of the time.

This also takes place when you write an essential letter, enjoy a movie or a video game, play chess or cards, or when you are engaged in any other activity that you enjoy doing, is unusual, or is delightful.

These examples show that a state of concentrated focus is feasible. However, real concentration is different. It is a more of a mindful and intentional process, in which, you focus your mind at will, whenever you desire, on whatever topic, for a certain period of time, not just for a couple of seconds.

Focus is the capability to focus the mind not just on pleasurable and also enjoyable issues and tasks that you enjoy, however likewise on your tasks and tasks, on your work or researches, and even on boring and uninteresting points that you require or have to do.

Why Concentration Is Important

This can be best answered by comparing your mind to a light bulb. The rays of the sun from the light bulb go out in all directions, and the energy spreads. If you stand 5 feet away from the bulb, you can see the light but can not really feel warm, also though there is wonderful warmth at the center of the bulb, at the filament. The primary resource of light requirement is not any type of higher than the light bulb we have simply reviewed, yet if you were to stand 5 feet from a laser beam of light resource, the beam would melt a whole right via your body.

In a similar way, concentrated thought likewise has world power. It has the potential of enhanced assumption, the ability to see even more of the underlying fact behind phenomena. It has the capacity to attain great things and to do unimaginable quantities of work. A focused mind is also an unwinded mind. Whenever you come to be deeply immersed in anything, you automatically pertain to a state of relaxation.

Since it avoids the mind from roaming aimlessly in all instructions, concentration is essential for everything that you do in life. Without focus, you can attain absolutely nothing. You only require to look around you to see the fact of this declaration.

Job finished with a focused mind becomes much more pleasurable. An individual with a focused mind can do all type of work with excellent performance. An individual who is not able to concentrate that considers other things while doing the operate at hand makes errors and takes an unneeded length of time to complete the task if he ever completes it in all. He will continuously consider how slowly the moment is passing. He will stress over himself, his problems, his family members, while he is functioning. As a result of inadequate concentration, there is an incomplete application, so the job is not correctly done. Focus is essential in day-to-day life and in the spiritual method.

Further, as Concentration is the capability to focus the attention on one only thought or topic, omitting every little thing else from the field of awareness.

The capability to focus the interest is one of the most crucial skills one needs to possess. Nevertheless, lots of people do not have the capacity to focus on. Their attention usually strays, without having the ability to repair it on one subject for any kind of reasonable time period.

This is something that can be fixed. The capacity to focus can be established, like any kind of other skill. An individual that educates his/her mind is able to concentrate, without being sidetracked by thoughts, noises or anything else.

Do you often ask yourself:

- Just how to be focused on researches?
- Just how to avoid making mistakes?
- Exactly how to be much more reliable?
- Just how to enhance memory?
- Just how to get results with affirmations?
- How to enhance the capacity to envision?

The solution is essential; you need to boost your ability to focus your attention.

WHY IS FOCUS IMPORTANT?

The importance of focus cannot be overstated. It is essential in every area of life and for everybody.

This ability can assist you when you require to be focused on your researches when you review, function, drive, get jobs done, meditate, and for everything else.

Focus and Concentration Are Important for:

1. Controlling your mind.

2. Turning down from your account the ideas that you do not desire.

3. Acquiring internal peace.

4. Releasing your mind from disturbing thoughts.

5. Improving your memory.

6. Improving your capacity to research.

7. Working more efficiently.

8. Making fewer mistakes.

9. Making progress with meditation.

10. Getting faster outcomes with creative visualization

11. Sharpening the intuition.

Insights and Benefits of Focus

A focused approach to issues pertaining to life brings a successful outcome. You know who is going to do well in assessments in a course at university because of just how concentrated the individual is. Focus is about what you spend most of your time thinking about and doing. A loss of emphasis can result in a loss of vision and inevitably a loss of everything you had ever before wished to be and have.

Samson(in the holy bible) never ever lost his eyes and hair and stamina up until he began tinkering women, Delilah and the woman of the street at Gaza being situations in the factor.

Think of your favourite artist, motion picture celebrity, preferred footballer right now, and I can inform you that the person you are thinking of is renowned because they did not choose to be everything to everyone.

1. Clearness of mind, and singleness of focus, is crucial to opening successful living in every element of one's life.

2. One cannot be wandering aimlessly every day and also at the end of the month and anticipate income or results without concentrating on vital result locations.

3. When those that purposely focused on their goals made points occur and relocated forward, wandering abstract principles will always end up questioning what happened.

4. A lack of focus will create you to wind up choosing what was not intended in the first place. No one purposely goes into a competition expecting to be a "runner up".

5. Bronze medals are meant for those that lost gold. What treasure are you missing out on out on because you lack accuracy in preparation?

6. Never ever enter into a meeting without an agenda, whether the one that required it has a plan or not. You will wind up regulating procedures because you are concentrated. Words "much" can be utilized as an acrostic/abbreviation for emphasis, activity and results.

7. Focused people go further because they do not play with their eyes on the scoreboard. They play with their eyes on the reward.

8. Concentrating daily over pay - off tasks will provide you success in the long run.

You can not be severe regarding a lot of various things that may negate and to attain phenomenal results. I use the "FAR" concept, that is, focus, activity, and results. What you continuously concentrate on you become, what you act on will positively identify what you obtain, which are your results. What are you focusing on today, this week or this month?

PASSIVE CONCENTRATION VERSUS ACTIVE CONCENTRATION

As you recognize, the focus is exceptionally vital in everybody's life, and it is just one of the primary factors for success or failure in all areas of life.

Many people discover it tough to focus their mind. However, there are times when they do concentrate, yet this is a passive concentration. Allow me to explain.

When you check out a fascinating book, do you often neglect everything else, and get completely immersed in the guide?

When you enjoy an excellent show or a good movie, do you often end up being unconcerned to every little thing else, also to hunger, your duties, or to the people around you?

When you participate in an activity that you like quite, do you forget about the time, and it appears to pass really quickly?

At such times you can overlook thoughts, sounds, people, discomfort and problems. It is as if the activity you have engaged it, draws your undivided interest, with no effort on your component. This is passive concentration.

Natural concentration is an automatic activity of the mind, launched via exterior elements; however, yet, it is concentration. This confirms that even people, that say they can not focus, actually can and do concentrate. This is not sufficient, considering that you also require to have energetic concentration.

Now you ask, what is an active concentration?

Making strategies, researching, doing something you never did previously, performing jobs and tasks that you wear' like doing, need interest, and concentrating on what you are doing. Getting ready for a test, doing something that you are not accustomed to doing or practising meditation, also calls for that you focus your focus. In all these instances, you might find it challenging to focus your mind.

When you do something, which you have to do, but don't like doing, you most likely discover it tough to maintain your mind concentrated. Due to the fact that your account keeps being sidetracked, you need to proactively and intently focus your mind.

Focusing your mind intently upon a particular idea, task or job, requires interest, self-control and willpower. This is a conscious act, and also you need to keep bringing your mind back repeatedly to the subject or task you are focusing on. This is an energetic focus.

Contrary to natural focus, active concentration needs initiative and aware interest.

Natural focus is relatively common and also is an automatic activity. It takes place when you are engaged in activities that you enjoy and also delights in doing, or there is some exterior variable that entirely attracts your interest. On these celebrations, the activity or external aspect manages your focus. It is not you, that willingly takes note.

This may appear harsh, but the mind can be trained to focus. A few minutes of focus exercises every day, in time, will create the ability to concentrate the mind on the job handy, an idea or an idea, even without effort. You will certainly be able to hold your account on one thought or topic, without being distracted, even for extended periods.

Just believe just how much energy and time you can conserve, and how much you can achieve when you develop active focus.

Easy exercise to train the mind to concentrate.

Count words in any type of one paragraph in a book or newspaper, and afterwards count them once more, to ascertain that you have actually counted them appropriately.

Exercise this workout daily, numerous times a day.

When this becomes very easy, attempt counting words in 2 paragraphs, and later, count words of an entire page.

To boost your focus and attention, count the words psychologically, only with your eyes, without pointing your finger at them.

This is a fundamental workout. Though an easy exercise, it may not be so straightforward to exercise, and you will find your mind straying and neglecting to count. This shows you how much you require to educate your concentration.

You utilize your mind every second of the day; however, you require to manage it, to focus it on what you are doing, and also this needs training the mind.

If you find this topic intriguing, and if you realize its relevance and also just how it can aid you with your day-to-day jobs and with accomplishing objectives

POWER OF CONCENTRATION

The power of concentration is the capability to concentrate the focus on one job or topic. Improving your powers of focus will assist you to get even more carried out in much less time. There are numerous advantages of this power and if used properly, can assist us to function carefully with our minds and also boost our lives. The power of focus is a psychological ability that has to be established, but when honed to razor-like intensity, its benefits are miraculous.

Below are several of the significant benefits of developing your ability to focus in addition to some practical actions for achieving severe concentration.

The Advantages of Improved Concentration:

1. Be extra effective: By dedicating your complete attention to whatever you're doing currently, you'll create far better high quality operate in less time. It really is this straightforward!

2. Be a far better good friend: Discussions are more positive if you seem like others are really listening to you. Focusing on others will aid you to value your friends and family, and understand exactly how to support them when they require it.

3. Really feel much more tranquil: Many kinds of research have discovered that multitasking makes people slower and much less reliable at performing various tasks. By comparison, focusing on one thing helps to calm your mind.

There are many benefits to creating the power of concentration. Below are a few of them:

- Control of your ideas.
- The ability to concentrate your mind
- Satisfaction.
- Flexibility from useless and bothersome ideas
- The capability to choose your ideas.
- Better memory.
- Boosted Confidence.
- Self-confidence.
- More powerful Willpower.
- Decisiveness.
- The capacity to study and understand quicker
- Internal joy.
- Much more reliable and effective use of creative visualization.
- Much more profound and new active meditation

And also far more.

TRAINING YOUR MIND TO CONCENTRATE

Concentrate on one thing at once: Place your mind on whatever you're carrying out in today moment. When you're engrossed in a thrilling movie or a brand-new romance and try to replicate that experience, assume concerning just how you act. Look for some significant facet or inspire yourself with the need to complete it in less time if you do not feel passionate about a certain job.

Abandon sidetracking ideas: Your mind will undoubtedly wonder. Continue to be aware of your thoughts. When you discover a distracting purpose, decrease to pursue it. Return your focus to your picked item. Repeat this as commonly as required. With practice, it will get less complicated.

Meditate: To enhance your development, try meditating. Sit and concentrate on your breath or spiritual accomplishments. You can extend that mindfulness to all your day-to-day tasks from consuming lunch to having fun with your children.

Other Steps to Improve Concentration:

1. Decrease external distractions: Your troubled mind is probably the best interruption, yet a controlled setting can assist too. If you can't discover a peaceful spot, consider utilizing white noise recordings, great songs, or earplugs.

2.Get fully engaged in what you're doing: It's less complicated to concentrate when you e proactively entailed. Take notes in course. Assume concerning questions you want to ask an audio speaker.

3. Vary your tasks: While you're increasing your attention span, it might be practical to change from one activity to another to stay alert. If you feel stuck writing a record, go return some phone telephone calls for a while - you'll really feel renewed when you come back to the record.

4. Plan routine breaks: Taking breaks can improve your efficiency. Conversation with your co-workers or walk around the block. Award yourself with an activity you enjoy after completing a hard project. Simply standing up from time to time is refreshing because it helps your mind obtain even more oxygen.

5. Avoid overloading your schedule: Budgeting your time really can make it easier to concentrate. You'll be much less likely to get sidetracked by concerns about getting whatever done.

6. Care for your wellness: Your physical health and wellness impacts all your psychological functioning. Obtain adequate rest and rest. Preserve a healthy and balanced weight by consuming a nutritious diet regimen and getting a daily workout.

Your capacity to focus will undoubtedly improve with practice. As you discover to concentrate more fully, you'll appreciate better peace of mind and also productivity.

HOW TO USE THE POWER OF CONCENTRATION

First, you need to understand a simple rule of life: Whatever you think about one of the most moderate increases in your life.

Some of the new masters are calling this the Regulation of Destination, and are treating it as if it is a new discovery. This is not brand-new; it is the method deep space was set up, in the beginning, to ensure that we people can be satisfied.

For example; if you are worried continuously regarding not having sufficient cash, you will certainly obtain even more life experiences of not having adequate money. What you consider the most will certainly show up right into your life as deep space responds to your wish by bringing right into your life what you have told it to.

This is just how deep space functions; what you think of the most is what the universe thinks you desire and also in order to make you pleased brings your need into your fact. Proceeding our example; focusing on chances to make cash will certainly get you further than fretting about the lack of it.

If you do not do anything, you will continue to be in your starving on the sofa state. You can focus, desire, and also will all you want. However, the food is not going to materialize right into your mouth. You will have to take some action to satisfy your cravings.

There are difficulties and tribulations in life. These occasions take place as seemingly random happenings; however, they come right into your life to assist you in expanding.

You can transform your ideas just by natural focus. You can catch yourself believing unfavourable, mad, absence of, inadequate, defeating thoughts and replace them with powerful ideas that work to further your goals in life. If you discover on your own assuming that there isn't adequate cash, you say to your self "AH HA" like you just busted your kid sneaking into the cookie jar, and after that state "waste" or "terminate" successfully disabling that idea. After that quickly replace it with something else that makes you delighted, like the thought of driving your Buzz via the countryside.

ACTION STEPS TO DEVELOP THE POWER OF CONCENTRATION TO MANIFEST YOUR DESIRES

Developing the power of concentration is an effective device for assisting you to solve whatever circumstance you're facing. Every problem has a remedy waiting to be discovered. However, this service many times requires the power of focus to produce the answer to you.

In this publication, we'll discover 3 action steps you can utilize now to create the power of focus to manifest your needs.

Action # 1 - Draw Up What You Need To be Fixed

Think of the goal you're working on and the area in which you're stuck. Throughout this process, recognize the location you're having success in and also the area you need resolution.

You may be focusing on your relationship with your partner, for example, and you will be useful in spending more time together, but there may be some friction in certain places when it comes to communication.

So you 'd write down

- success area = spending more time together
- the area that needs working on = far better communication

Or if you're servicing an organization, one location might show to be efficient while development appears to be stunted in another. Accurately, determine these locations as received the example over.

Action # 2 - Visualize Your Result

Since you have actually clearly identified the location, you need to service, plainly define what you 'd such as completion result to be. You see, you're checking out where you are currently and where you need to be, so you have a clear target that you're functioning towards.

Making use of the partnership example over, you recognized that you and also your companion is not open up enough in your communication, or you shout instead of talk with each other when dealing with more extreme circumstances. What would certainly your desired results be?

Activity Step # 3 - Get Inspired Concepts To Manifest Your Preferred Outcome

Below's where the majority of people get stuck since they don't recognize just how to obtain from where they are to where they need to be. At this moment, you'll use 2 tools to get yet.

> **Tool #1 - Use your observational skills**

What causes the breakdown in communication? What are you performing in your service that's not functioning? Think of the last time you attempted to communicate what happened? What set off the debate? As you use your observational abilities to emotionally observe your very own actions which of your partner or to observe your service, you'll begin to see patterns that activate certain responses and results.

> ### **Tool #2 - Use the Law of Thinking**

Currently, begin to turn on the Regulation of Believing. You identified the issue, and you utilized your empirical abilities to figure out where you're obtaining the snags in your partnership, service or whatever objective you're servicing, currently, through the Regulation of Assuming, brainstorm possible options to settle the circumstance. Write these down.

Apply your best suggestions but keep an open mind and pay attention within for various other inspired ideas that surface from within you. Likewise, provide room to permit things to unravel usually also. When you start this process, it's amazing how things are set in motion and start functioning quickly and seamlessly as you move on to your favourite outcomes because, transforming your life may appear like an overwhelming, frustrating process. It does not have to be if you're offered simple, manageable detailed strategies that will certainly obtain you from where you are to where you want to be and also experience a transformed life.

The Power Of Thought Concentration Creates Circumstances

When we are faced with problems in our fate, we can utilize a tool kit of powers and faculties with which to change occasions and conditions. Despite exterior conditions, we can release forces within ourselves that slowly cause darkness and also obscurity to vanish.

An essential means through which we can harness our inner pressures for optimum advantage is with focus as concentration is the focusing of psychological concentrate on a particular subject. It might be contrasted to the power of a magnifying glass to focus on the rays of the sunlight. Equally, as a magnifying glass can melt an opening via timber or stir up a fire so can the concentrated mind permeate to the option of an issue or spark originalities and understandings.

Concentration is vital to any kind of creative minds work. Control of assuming implements the high state of linking ourselves with the great consciousness. When we can concentrate the mind at will, this state of greater understanding, cosmic awareness, or absorption in nature is only feasible. Just with the mental focus can we maintain the frequencies of a higher degree of consciousness.

Focus resembles a laser which enhances light right into a single light beam of incredible power. Basically, a laser is a ruby pole surrounded by a spiral light. When the sun gets on the chromium atoms of the ruby are promoted. When the excitement is entirely fantastic, a slim beam of light of sufficient sun prolongs from the ruby crystals.

The spiral lamp which boosts or excites the chromium atoms in the ruby rod may be contrasted to our feelings. When we are adequately interested in something, our excitement stimulates the molecules of our mind represented by the ruby pole. By focusing on the light of our objectives and our dreams via mental focus, we can achieve exceptional results very rapidly.

When we really feel passionate concerning something the act of psychological focusing will itself stir up interest and enthusiasm in any idea of the study, not just is focus induced a lot more quickly

The power of focus is a magical tool that we can develop or damage depending upon the topic of bad attention and the nature of our ideas. The saying of the Buddha "enduring complies with a bad thought as the wheels of the cart follow the oxen that attract it and joy follow a great idea like the darkness that never leaves".

When you focus your mind on a visual scenario, you are concentrating right into your area of experience, and the extreme scenes you picture. For every psychological reason, there follows a physical outcome; and positive ideas will undoubtedly produce like results. What the mind develops, it eventually receives so long as the intention is stable enough.

Is The Power Of Concentration Really Needed To Achieve Success?

Isn't it fascinating how quickly we have the ability to concentrate on something that is harmful and adverse, however, have a tough time holding on to ideas - for any type of size of time - when it's something helpful?

Attempt it. Try to consider one advantage now that makes you rejoice, excited or secure. Hold that idea and also the vision for 5 minutes.

Nearly challenging to do, wasn't it? Possibly your mind kept wandering to a list of jobs that you need to get completed or slides back to a current problem that's been worrying you recently.

Now, take into consideration how typically you think about issues that annoy you, make you angry or sad, every single day. A few of them can consume you for days!

When was the last time a happy, constructive thought held your focus for days? Exactly how around someday? Okay, you must have the ability to think about one that kept you smiling for a minimum of an hour, right?

You could come up with an instance of one, couldn't you? Just for an hr, one delighted, thrilled idea that had you smiling, without any negative thoughts intruding?

Did you ever before stop to assume what an integral part of your ideas - focused thoughts - play in your life?

Think it or not, but it's "you" that selects what you focus your thoughts on. Only "you" can choose to cut and also throw the button off the circulation of power right into unfavourable opinions. Only "you" can make a decision to focus on constructive and uplifting thoughts.

In order to make a success of anything in your life, you should be able to concentrate your entire idea upon the idea that you are working on. Allowing disturbances, uncertainties, or stress to get in and also regulate your mind will take power away, and cause you to lose concentrate on what you intend to achieve.

When you shed that focus, you begin to fall behind on what you had planned to do. You might come up with all kinds of factors why you obtained distracted or why you just "had to believe" concerning a particular issue.

Focused focus, and activity, are needed to attain success - in any part of your life. Letting your mind drift willy nilly and also assessing devastating thoughts will only keep you stuck exactly where you are currently.

Has residence on any type of adverse thoughts assisted you in any kind of method? Precisely what has it completed other than to make you miserable and mad?

Concentrating on wrong things, holding onto unfavourable thoughts, does not accomplish anything except to make you really feel even worse than you currently really feel. Focus on the existing and also what great things you desire to achieve right now, in this minute.

That's where success exists.

Which ideas do you select to focus on?

How to Unleash Your Power of Concentration?

It's one of the most powerful success approaches of them all! Even more success and also a ton of money have actually been attributed to large focus or instead focus than any type of various other success methods around. Why?

Well, the fact of the issue is that there many of us have beautiful concepts and hopes of success in our lives or companies.

It starts as sparkling in your eye after obtaining an inspiring advertising message or some incredible suggestion that pertained to you in the shower or some other place where your mind was cost-free to assume without distraction. The issue is that when it boils down to actually obtaining it done, we typically fail because of things like laziness, interruptions, insecurity, variance and even are afraid.

The unfavourable fact is that the world is literally littered with the "carcasses" of deserted suggestions and potential success that never ever came true for the essential factor that the individual behind them ended up being unfocused, put things off, or began to doubt the validity of their concept in the first place.

Think of this:

" Star Wars" has become one of the most lucrative films and item franchise business in the background, however, the fact is, at that time the basic concept of "Celebrity Wars" was declined by every motion-picture studio in Hollywood prior to 20th Century Fox approved it! Can you envision that?

With the straightforward power of focus, George Lucas was able to single-mindedly to progress via consistent being rejected and also generate the legendary "Star Wars" films that have actually been launched from 1977 to 2005. (I think even more ahead).

Fact is, this is not an original case. There are countless stories of victory and also accomplishment, fame and wealth because of Emphasis.

Currently, there are straightforward steps any individual can require to really attain success via focus.

Three easy steps truly

1. Locate and specify a specific objective for your idea or desire: Realize that desires, and suggestions, will come and go, but, it only takes ONE concept or wish to accomplish success. Everybody at some time in their lives has a lot of suggestions and also not nearly enough time to achieve them all. Pick the one you are most passionate about.

2. Form the habit of concentrating on that one idea or desire without allowing distraction: You should control your impulses, interests, emotions, actions and also inadequate routines. If not, you will undoubtedly wind up tossing yet one more carcass in the ditch of failure. Just and habitually, seek to manage those things as you pursue your idea or need. Questioning to boost your suggestion is fine, however challenging to find a reason to stop is what the majority of us do all frequently. Keep in mind, the turf does not regularly look green day-to-day, and there will undoubtedly be times that you question your very own actions. Utilize them intelligently and with development in mind.

3. Build and strengthen your thoughts and mind as you work toward fulfilling your idea or desire: Various ideas, and people, are always amongst us. There are always good ones and bad ones in both. As you work towards accomplishment, your ideas and mind need to collaborate with positive power in order to conquer your individual and also psychological enemies. (that would be negative thoughts and people).

Sticking and complying with to these 3 actions is the right course of a champion.

It is of miraculous worth to discover how to focus. To make the greatest success of anything, you must be able to concentrate your entire thought upon the idea you are working with. The person that is able to focus makes use of all constructive ideas and locks out all harmful ones. The best man would certainly achieve nothing if he did not have focus." Through emphasis or the power of concentration, ANY INDIVIDUAL can attain greatness on an impressive range.

Consider it is "Focus" the real "Pressure"?

Become a Master of Focus, and you WILL achieve greatness and prosperity!

LACK OF CONCENTRATION AND FOCUS

Individuals often ask me what to do to boost their concentration. It seems that lack of concentration is a widespread issue, regardless of gender, age or nation.

What people say about the lack of concentration

- " I attempt to concentrate; however, I soon find myself thinking of another thing."
- " It is hard for me to focus my interest when I research."
- " My mind maintains going from one idea to an additional."
- " When I attempt to concentrate on what I am doing, quickly, my ideas frequently drift to other points."
- " I cannot finish what I start doing."
- " I do not have a concentration. I am not able to focus my mind on something for greater than a couple of seconds."

- " I typically procrastinate, since I cannot concentrate for long, and then drop what I am doing."

These are simply a few of the things individuals' say. The common thread of all these declarations is the lack of focus and the failure to focus the mind on one point each time. Lack of concentration affects work, partnerships, college, and also virtually every little thing else.

Occasionally, the problem is severe and may need clinical focus and also recommendations. If you are an average person, do not have concentration; however, have no wellness issues as the reason for the lack of focus, you can fix this situation by exercising concentration exercises.

In this age of the internet, mobile phones, social media networks and info overload, the trouble is also more significant. They make the interest period even much shorter.

Do you really feel that you do not have concentration?

Do you feel that you lack sufficient focus, and would like to enhance it?

Lack of focus seems to be extremely common, especially nowadays, with numerous disturbances, a lot of info, gizmos, advertising and marketing, and products that attract your attention in a lot of ways.

This takes place anywhere, at the workplace, at college and also at home. Walking, consuming, working out, studying, and even nearly task, are performed with a divided focus, and consequently, not so efficiently, and at the threat of making mistakes and mistakes.

What is concentration? It is the capability to manage the attention, select on what to focus it, and decline unimportant ideas and also diversions. It allows you to come to be the master of your mind and not the opposite.

This is an ability, which requires to be acquired, and calls for some job. It resembles finding out to swim, to drive or to dance. You do not get these skills just by considering them. You need technique over a period of time.

Ask Yourself:

- Is your focus all right, or do you assume it needs renovation?
- In which area of your life do you need it most?
- Do you genuinely wish to reinforce this capability?
- Do you conveniently focus on your work, research studies, or anything else that requires interest, or do you find it tough to control your attention?
- Is your mind in constant internal chatter?
- If you are making use of imaginative visualization or affirmations, do you feel that you require to improve your capacity to concentrate your mind?

If you were given workouts and guidelines to enhance your ability to concentrate, would you follow and also exercise them?

You can fix your lack of focus, by learning to focus your concentration. You require a particular degree of self-control to do that.

If you are earnest enough, you will possibly notice some improvement within a few weeks, and also as you go on, your capacity will certainly remain to expand. With practice, this skill would improve.

Common Causes of a Lack of Concentration

Keep in mind when you remained in elementary school and you had a crush on some lovable schoolmate? All you did throughout the day was stare right into area and doodle his/her name on your notebook while the teacher stood at the front of the classroom lecturing on the essential days in history that you needed to find out for your history examination. This is a lack of focus that the majority of us have actually experienced in the past and still do under some conditions today.

There have most likely been times where you merely could not get your mind on the task at hand. You might have had something else more crucial on your account or only lacked the interest in what you were attempting to do to allow you to maintain your focus. While this type of absence of attention is typical for anybody, for others, it can be a signs and symptom of a clinical condition.

In the exact same way that "flu-like signs and symptoms" are the exact same for a number of various illnesses, a lack of concentration can have a whole lot of multiple causes. Chronic tiredness that results from a number of different reasons can cause an absence of focus that continues for an extensive period of time.

Any type of kind of trauma to the head or a disease that influences the mind can trigger an absence of concentration. While an injury is something that the person is ordinarily aware of, conditions like mind lumps or hematomas (embolism) might not be quickly evident. Both prescription and illicit medicines can create a lack of focus for different periods after use depending upon the details medication and the length of time it continues to be in your body.

The reality is that there are actually hundreds of causes of a lack of concentration that prolong from harmless, typical ones to those that are far more major. However, the majority of people that suffer from an absence of focus as a result of severe anxiety are not likely to seek the aid they need because of their problem. It can specify that they rest and gaze blankly at the tv throughout the day!

One more trouble with the regularity you may experience an absence of concentration is that you might believe you know what is creating it when, in fact, there is a much more significant factor for it. While depression is probably the most cited cause of a lack of concentration, there is no assurance that this is the factor for yours. As a matter of fact, you may have an additional issue that is triggering both the anxiety and also the absence of focus. The possibility for an extreme condition is substantial enough that if you have a lack of concentration, it is critical that you obtain taken a look at by a physician to establish the cause.

Obstacles to Concentration

Do you find it challenging to hold your focus fixed on one topic or assumed longer than a couple of seconds, prior to obtaining sidetracked by various other ideas or feeling impacts? There are numerous obstacles to concentration that everyone deals with, yet these challenges can be overcome.

What are the obstacles to focus?

- Lack of sufficient self-discipline
- Lack of enough self-discipline
- Impatience.
- Unrestrained mind.
- Excessive rate of interest in various other ideas
- Physical and psychological restlessness.
- Absence of understanding what concentration is.
- Lack of ability to rest still
- Disease.
- Lack of inspiration to improve the focus.
- Much tension and lack of adequate rest.

There are other obstacles to concentration, but these are the main ones.

In order to get rid of these obstacles to focus, you need to create and reinforce your determination and self-discipline through suitable workouts.

Thinking frequently about the advantages of obtaining the ability to concentrate and concentrate your mind can assist as well, and duplicating affirmations concerning your wish to improve this capacity. This will strengthen your motivation and need and assist you in conquering the challenges en route.

Practising some physical exercises throughout the day will enhance your health and also your capability to conquer physical uneasiness. It is likewise crucial to learn to offer on your own some remainder during the day and offer on your own sufficient rest in the evening.

Attempt to remain calm and also relaxed during the day, regardless of what occurs.

Showing some inner detachment would help. Do not allow on your own be as well impacted by what individuals do or state, and also don't let external influences change your state of minds and state of mind.

If you let people and also exterior events influence your moods and frame of mind, how can you concentrate your mind when you need to? It holds true, it could not be easy to remove this habit, yet if you discover to be aware of this subconscious behaviour, you will gradually be able to weaken its effect on you.

Obviously, do not fail to remember that you also need to find some time every day to exercise focus workouts.

Hypnotherapy or listening to unique CDs could assist and also bring some fast outcomes, yet lasting and genuine results come via gradual work and even by establishing the mental muscle mass, and not through outside methods.

Aware and gradual growth, create in the future, far better and also long-lasting outcomes. It resembles taking tablets and hormonal agents to develop physical strength and muscular tissues versus exercising real physical exercises. It might take longer and calls for some effort, but the incentives are enjoyable and worthwhile.

You can conquer the obstacles to concentration if you really want to do so. They will not vanish overnight, however eventually, they will.

How to Overcome Lack of Concentration

In today's circumstance when interruptions are simply a click away in the type of social media networks, messages or emails, it is without a doubt under how one obtains any job done properly. In the meanwhile, it really easy for one to lose emphasis also like the focus period ends up being also shorter.

Currently, lack of concentration might likewise cause the individual not doing one's task well. It needs to be altered.

This short article goes over some factors on exactly how to get over a lack of focus at the workplace.

Why Overcome Lack of Concentration?

One has realized that there are several reasons why there is a need to get over the absence of focus at work. If a person sheds focus on work, it can cause one making stupid errors such as emailing some vital work, while failing to remember to connect the related files and even neglecting to make that urgent telephone call, when called for.

One more example is additionally of when one neglected what to create, while in the midst of a vital message. The job would certainly experience when the person loses focus or is not able to concentrate well on duty. It is common enough expertise that a person who can focus well or focus on the work effectively can take place to do one's job truly well.

Tips To Overcome Lack Of Concentration:

In the meantime, one might have seen circumstances where one was deeply fascinated by whatever they were doing, like in reading, playing musical instruments or playing a video game and so forth. It is possible to obtain that equal focus for job Look at ways to get over a lack of concentration.

- **Why should you do it?**

When somebody cannot be troubled to complete an activity, there is every chance that can get tired and also shed concentration. If the task is boring or boring, it is all-natural for the people to request the reason, on why a job is being done? Or instead on purposed it?

One can be researching a subject, that is not of the rate of interest to the person with the objective to a rating in the tests and also, therefore, land a desired job. Or could be that is associated with some boring and tedious task with the objective to add to the growth or growth of one's firm.

Whatever be the cause for doing the job, one point to comprehend is that when one has a factor to complete the work, the person might conveniently get inspired and thus will be able to concentrate well and complete the job on schedule.

- **Strategize well**

There might be many circumstances when one jumped right into some work, just to be completely perplexed and weighed down under expectations. What one requires to understand is that some work needs to be done in order. One can not intend to begin from the middle of some work and proceed with no obstacle.

Therefore, it is called for that an individual must organize the jobs. Take place and see to it that the tasks to be done are prepared in order. One would certainly require to see which would come first. See to it to also see if any type of data is missing. As is organized, one can relocate ahead without any problem if one follows through with the strategy. It is seen that pausing in between to see what follows, also makes one lose emphasis.

- **Work for short periods**

One could think that taking breaks could help one to concentrate much more on their work, quickly. When one breaks in between, it is likewise evident that working for short term functions much better. Nobody can ever go on to concentrate for a long period of time, at a stretch.

Once, you have been at work for regarding half an hr or more in one go, and there is a demand to pause and charge one's powers. At the same time, people remain on work and also focus well, once they have the break to anticipate within a specified time.

For example, one can opt to do the work for half an hour approximately, with a break being available in between prior to one resumes the job again. At the very same time, if one attempted to operate at one go for two or 3 hrs, one could be losing concentration every 10 minutes or two.

- **Keep your door shut**

Every office without a doubt has a door. How lots of individuals do really decide to keep it closed? While hectic on duty, it is far better to shut the door, so regarding tell everybody that the person is active and would not like to be interrupted.

If functioning from home, after that definitely choose this alternative to ensure that one's focus is not in any way interrupted by one's family members, for instance by partner or children. It would certainly also be better if one might inform that there should not be any kind of interruption as one can be hectic. One can additionally take place to choose earphones to block off any kind of more diversions.

- **Eat moderately**

Because the individual could get conveniently bothered, one should never go starving while on the task. It is seen that when the blood sugar drops, the person could shed focus and will have an attention deficit disorder. One can also remain in an awful frame of mind.

At the very same time, if an individual is to eat well and load one's belly, then one would certainly feel sluggish and slow. One should take care to consume reasonably.

For lunch, instead of having a heavy lunch, have a sandwich or something light like a grain bar or fruit to eat.

- ## **Cut off-Web Connection**

Well, with the social media sites networks, emails and also other things on the web waiting for a person to come in, it gets simple for one to lose focus. It is discovered that whenever one obtains online to examine social networks sites such as Facebook, Twitter, or so on, it takes them time to leave it and also get back to work.

When this happens, one likewise often tends to lose concentrate on the work. Hence, unless the internet is required for the individual to do the job, it is better that opts to have it off.

- ## **Go Slow**

It is inevitable that one would lose concentration. Whenever anyone is in a hurry running around getting things done. In such situations, the individual would certainly additionally wind up making more errors. At the very same time, when one attempts to repair it, even more time is spent on it.

If ever before one has made some error, which takes a person's job, like sending an incorrect mail or neglecting vital things, then the entire experience could be a failure. However, if one was to take things individually at recreation, the individual will be able to concentrate more and, therefore, be a lot more qualified and also obtain more points done on schedule.

• **Do a difficult job when you are alert**

One would also need to understand, exactly how to organize one's service the basis of the energy degrees. That is if one opts to do the hardest job, each time when one is most attentive, then it needs to aid to make the most of one's concentration.

• **Schedule Email downloads**

It is seen that emails can take place to interrupt the concentration of the person at the office. Most of the individuals are attracted to address the inbound emails in between tasks. If we can schedule the emails coming into a few times in a day, one can also opt to deal with all mails at one go.

- ### Make the best use of Rest

Rest is really essential for every person. Absence of proper sleep can leave one really cranky, sluggish and tired, therefore causing the absence of concentration, while at the workplace.

Determine the factor for absence of rest, and reasons could be numerous fold including depression, anxiety at the workplace or house, odd work hours or other wellness conditions.

When the trouble is determined, go on to discover the option. Attempt and obtain optimal rest, so that one can come back the lost concentration. To get rest, one would certainly need to avoid high levels of caffeine, have a cosy shower, listen to music or even check out a publication.

General suggestions to manage the absence of focus:

There could be many reasons for lack of concentration. It could also be the symptom of other conditions such as depression, menopause, anxiety, pregnancy, deficit disorder, chronic fatigue, and so on. If the symptom persists, one may need to consult the physician about this. Some other common tips on how to overcome lack of concentration are to resort to meditation, eat balanced meals filled with nutrition, exercise regularly, get plenty of sleep, shut off all distractions at work and much more. One can also listen to music if it would help someone to concentrate.

10 Ways to Increase Your Concentration

1. Recognize what concentration is: "Focus is taking your mind off several things and also putting it on one point at once." Typically what distracts us are day-to-day misunderstandings and also negative feelings.

2. Choose what you intend to focus on: In several methods, you become what you focus on-- that is, you take on several of its attributes. Have you ever before observed how couples who have been married for years begin to look like each various other, or exactly how people often come to resemble their pet dogs, their vehicles, their hobbies, or their job jobs?

3.   Enjoy   various   other   individuals concentrating: Go see an excellent activity motion picture. It would undoubtedly make a really significant distraction to damage their attention stream. These physical signs may provide you with a hint regarding means to boost your very own focus abilities.

4. Prevent continuous sensory input: Multi-tasking (attempting to do greater than one thing each time), loud sounds, and aesthetic excitement (such as from a T.V.) making focus a lot more challenging, and being around them or doing them way too much can put you into a routine of non-attention which can be tough to break.

5. Make it a point to put your complete concentration on whatever you are doing: Don't allow anything to distract you. It actually assists to be in a quiet area, but you can discover to shut out noise if needed.

6. Learn to meditate: Meditation is the most powerful of all focus enhancement techniques. Discover a few natural meditation methods and practise them at least five minutes daily.

7. Learn techniques to increase and control your energy: One such strategy is Paramhansa Yogananda'sEnergization Workouts. Regulating your power is an essential very first step towards the capacity to focus intensely.

8. Take breaks: Go outdoors and breathe deeply or take a brisk walk. Make yourself do this usually, and you'll be able to go back to your job charged and ready to focus even more artistically.

9. Stay calm: Deep concentration is a matter of increasing or directing your life-force or conscious, cosmic energy. The more of this kind of energy you have, the better. Scattered energy doesn't help. It must be calm, focused energy. Learn to be calmly concentrated and be gentle.

10. While practising meditation, watch your breath: Do not manage it in any way, simply observe. This educates you to focus your mind on something at a time. As you keep your breath, it will undoubtedly decrease, together with your mind, and you move right into a vibrant, peaceful (yet not drowsy) state of being.

FACTORS THAT AFFECT FOCUS AND CONCENTRATION

When it's functioning well, our capability to concentrate and focus allows us to achieve incredible points--. Interruptions are the primary factor we lose emphasis, yet frequently these aren't as evident as you may picture.

Rather, you might feel scattered or "unclear" or blame yourself for not having even more control.

As we get older, emphasis and also focus can alter, as can memory and other cognitive features, however, this is not unpreventable. Some studies with older individuals reveal no decline in decision-making capabilities, and the ability for calculated learning-- using particular methods to recognize something-- can also obtain much better with age. Individuals in their 70s can be "a lot more diligent and cautious, without being hyper-vigilant" than those in their 50s.

If you have lousy focus, you might feel as if you merely need to try harder, but this strategy probably will not aid. Instead, you can have a much better emphasis by acting to advertise renovations in the particular mind functions that drive concentration and understanding.

By developing the conditions that make it much easier to focus and also complete your work, you can really feel sharper and much more focused, especially when you have a particular task to achieve.

Look through these variables that affect emphasis-- for better or worse-- and also keep in mind of how many apply to you. Beginning at any of these points can be your initial step toward having far better concentration and focus for every little thing you do.

FACTORS THAT HINDER FOCUS

Poor diet and nutrition

Fat burning diets are infamously negative for focus. Since the brain requires particular essential fatty acids, low-fat diet regimens can mess up emphasis. But not getting sufficient healthy protein is bad as well. The amino acids in protein are essential for creating key mind chemicals used for focus. Refined foods cause blood glucose spikes and accidents that ruin emphasis. And if you do not obtain essential vitamins (specifically B vitamins and vitamin D) and also minerals, consisting of appropriate iron, your capability to concentrate will experience, and also it will certainly aggravate gradually.

Hunger

Hunger is an interruption we've all had. Several studies show the unfavourable effects that cravings carry young grownups and school-aged youngsters. Appetite is connected directly to reduced blood glucose which swiftly leads to exhaustion and low power levels-- and also all ruin your ability to focus.

Dehydration

Loss of emphasis is the precise adverse effect of not consuming alcohol sufficient water and also researches verify it. Dehydration can likewise bring about other signs that consequently lower emphasis, consisting of frustration signs and symptoms, tiredness, and reduced state of mind. Also having just 1% less than optimum hydration can create a lack of focus.

Hormonal changes

Regular hormonal fluctuations and shifts, like those while pregnant or menopause, can affect just how well women focus. This is so common during the midlife change that loss of focus is thought about a signs and symptom of menopause by many health care practitioners.

Lack of rest

This is a big one since if you don't get adequate rest-- also for simply one evening-- your thought processes can reduce, you're yawnless, sharp than normal and your capacity to concentrate suffers. You can become so confused that you can't do jobs calling for a complex idea. If you're drowsy and that additionally, impacts focus negatively, it's also hard to remember and also learn brand-new points. Insufficient rest likewise reduces right into working memory, an important part of concentrating. It makes you less vigilant and also lowers both your precision and speed on psychological jobs. If your sleep issues become chronic and long-term-- something numerous individuals struggle with-- your reduced ability to focus can become your new typical, which can adversely affect your work, connections and also personal growth.

Stress

Stress is unpreventable, but it can have alarming repercussions on focus and focus if it ends up being persistent. Job concerns, partnership issues and also wellness worries can make it difficult to concentrate, though great deals of people do not see this taking place till they become totally overloaded. If you have to reread points a great deal since you cannot concentrate, your work may not get done, and also of training course, that alone causes also extra tension.

Medical, emotional and psychological problems

Any kind of serious concern that influences your health, psychological or physical, can harm your emphasis, including sleep apnea, toxicity from heavy steels, terrible mind injury, stroke,

ADHD, finding out specials needs, aesthetic problems, dementia, anxiousness, depression, bipolar disorder, and psychological injury.

Lack of exercise

You won't understand exactly how deeply your capability to focus is impacted up until you actually get relocating if you don't work out. As an example of just how the mind takes advantage of workout, one study revealed that three months of the cardio exercise was linked to the creation of new neurons, and more comprehensive and deeper interconnections in between them. These sorts of neuronal improvements can reinforce and also boost concentration.

Your environment

Is it too peaceful or also loud when you're attempting to focus? Is your atmosphere loaded with distractions like ringing phones, humming light fixtures, rattling heater vents, or aesthetic interruptions? Maybe it's also warm-- or also cold. Just how around your comfort level (chair, work desk elevation, lights)? Are people constantly interrupting you? Every one of these elements can influence emphasis.

High quality of details

It's complicated to harness your emphasis if you do not have the appropriate information to work with. An insufficient email, a deceptive phone message or a skipped step along the method can muddle your focus as you attempt to make sense of the small details.

FACTORS THAT IMPROVE FOCUS

Good Diet

You can improve your ability to focus greatly by changing your diet plan toward consuming healthy foods from the Mediterranean-style of consuming.

Regularly eating foods that sustain healthy and balanced mind function increases focus and can also aid you to have more persistence with disturbances.

Along with modest quantities of lean protein, fill your plate with great deals of veggies and fruit. Add entire grains and also use olive oil to prepare rather than butter.

Consume a good breakfast to send a message to your body that it's going to obtain the fuel it requires-- you will certainly be much less worried literally and much better able to remain concentrated.

Key Nutrients and Foods For Focus

- **Vitamin B3 or niacin--** required to maintain the continuous supply of sugar that your brain makes use of for energy. Without it, you're likely to fight with bad focus, complication and also memory loss. Access least 20mg a day.

- **Vitamin B6—**necessary to produce neurotransmitters and avoid complications and concentration deficiency. Use 20 mg daily.

- **Vitamin B12--** B12 is a crucial component for having a healthy myelin sheath around the nerves. B12 shortage is rather typical-- it influences at the very least 15% of grownups over 60-- and it's preventable. Aim for 1000mcg daily.

- **Vitamin B5 or pantothenic acid-**essential for the oxidative metabolism (the first phase of the metabolic process) of sugar and fats, and for the synthesis of fats, acetylcholine, cholesterol and melatonin; Go with at least 20mg per day.

- **Vitamin C**-- this effective anti-oxidant assists make the natural chemical norepinephrine, which services the part of your brain where the focus is managed.

- **Curcumin**-- this unique polyphenol from turmeric extract has actually been made use of for generations to "properly manage stress in China," according to the US federal government's National Center for Biotechnology Information. More recent studies recommend curcumin can boost the birth of new mind cells, which is necessary for ideal knowing, and advertise connections to various other brain cells while shielding them from damages. Also, small amounts of dietary turmeric extract are linked to lower prices of mental deterioration. As a powerful antioxidant, curcumin tamps down the swelling that adds to mental decline. Considering that curcumin is difficult for the body to take in, labs can make use of black pepper to enhance its absorption and also bioavailability by as high as 2000%, making it easy to get the quantity you need daily. Take as long as 450mg of curcumin every day.

- **Quercetin**-- an additional active ingredient with secure antioxidant homes, quercetin is a flavonoid or a sort of plant pigment that aids provide veggies and fruits their dazzling shade. Research shows that it can help with complimentary radicals and inflammation.

Targeted Supplemental Nutrition

Research study has actually already identified many of the essential nutrients and active ingredients that straight sustain brain features like emphasis and focus. The series of B vitamins, and also particularly B12, b6, and also b9, are definitely important for good focus. Vitamin D is also a vital nutrient, and also choline has terrific science behind it for mental wellness. The current exploration with solid study sustaining it is curcumin, an active plant ingredient derived from turmeric that has powerful anti-inflammatory homes. Antioxidant ingredients like quercetin can likewise aid with swelling.

Avoiding getting hungry

Eat regular dishes, with at the very least two wholesome treats in between. Appetite is sidetracking and signals that your mind isn't obtaining the power it needs to sustain emphasis and concentration. Do not eat hearty or overly abundant foods-- they can have a sedating effect.

Ideal foods for emphasis-- these choices are recognized to support or enhance focus and concentration.

- Leafy green veggies like spinach can increase signals between nerve cells to make your mind a lot more responsive.
- Omega 3 rich foods like salmon, walnuts and also pumpkin seeds are superb for brain health and wellness and concentrating ability.oil
- Eggs-- yolk and white together-- include brain-supporting choline and also phenylalanine that your body makes use of to produce the neurotransmitter

dopamine. Eggs are likewise an excellent source of the omega-3 DHA.

- Avocados have monounsaturated fats that support healthy and balanced blood circulation.
- Whole grains help boost blood circulation, control glucose (consistent glucose levels make it a lot easier to concentrate) and also decrease the danger of plaque developing in the brain.
- Blueberries can boost discovering while shielding the brain from cost-free radicals.

Plenty of water

One of the most important steps you can take to help ensure good focus is after getting enough water in your body throughout the day. Thirst isn't the best measure of fluid status, so lack of focus can be a significant early dehydration indicator. Dr Sharon Stills, ND, has a smart way to find out how much water is good for you: drink half your weight every day in ounces.

Right environment

It's important to set yourself up for great emphasis by picking and adjusting your environments as needed. Find the very best location in your house to concentrate, or transfer to a coffee or the collection shop if that fits your design better. Too much silence can drive a lot of people crazy-- believe holding cell. And if it is as well quiet, you'll hear every little disruptive noise, so aim for a little history noise. On the other hand, if you're combating too much sound, attempt noise-cancelling headphones or create white noise with a follower. Paying attention to non-distracting songs can aid-- try gentle or classical electronic tunes.

Good sleep every night

Simply as vital as the food you eat, is sleep-- both are basic elements of good brain function. Obtain seven hours of sleep per night or up to 9 hours on event. For most of us, anything much less than 7 hrs eats into a certain phase recognized as delta, or slow-wave sleep, which will certainly make it difficult to concentrate when we're awake.

Get your game on

Brain video games might not be the only type of game that can help enhance concentration. More recent research likewise suggests playing video games might assist boost concentration.

A 2018 research taking a look at 29 people found proof to suggest an hr of pc gaming can help improve visual selective attention (VSA). VSA describes your ability to focus on a specific job while disregarding interruptions around you.

This research study was limited by its small size, so these findings aren't definitive. The research also really did not determine how much time this boost in VSA lasted.

Research study authors recommend future research to continue exploring just how video games can help increase brain task and also increase focus.

A 2017 review trusted Resource checked out 100 studies taking a look at the effects video games might carry cognitive function. The outcomes of the testimonial suggest playing video games might lead to various modifications in the mind, including increased interest and emphasis.

This testimonial had numerous constraints, consisting of the reality that the studies concentrated on commonly differing subjects, including video game dependency and the possible results of violent computer game. Researches mainly created to explore the benefits of a computer game can assist support these findings.

Exercise

Exercise can make wonderful points for focus: simply one session can enhance psychological emphasis and cognitive efficiency for any kind of task you're trying to complete. One research showed that also if individuals have attention deficits, they can hone their emphasis with a physical task because it releases brain chemicals connected with knowing and memory. A short, intense session of running in place speeds flow to the brain and improves emphasis quick.

Listen to music

Activating songs while functioning or examining might assist boost focus. Even if you don't enjoy listening to songs while you function, using nature audios or white sound to mask history sounds might additionally aid concentration and other brain features, according to study. The sort of music you pay attention to can make a distinction. Experts normally agree on classical music, especially baroque classical music or nature audios are good selections to help increase your emphasis.

If you don't care for classical music, attempt ambient or digital songs without lyrics, keep the music soft, or at background sound level, so it does not end up distracting you. It's also essential to stay clear of choosing songs you like or hate, considering that both kinds can wind up sidetracking you.

Stress reduction

You can limit the effects of stress and anxiety on your capability to focus by just taking a break at noontime and doing definitely nothing for a solid 5mins. Pausing literally disrupts the pattern of stress-building and also can help you recover your emphasis, or prevent it from being lost.

Excellent breathing

Do you unconsciously hold your breath, especially when focusing intensely on a comprehensive project or fine-motor job? Make also much more effective changes to your focus with deep stomach breathing: area one hand on your belly and inhale for 3 full seconds and feel your belly increase, and after that exhale for 3secs pressing the air out with your belly muscles, feeling your tummy drop. Add meditation to your deep breathing method-- also for just 30secs-- to re-focus your brain in the face of distractions.

Have a little caffeine

Obtain a short-lived boost to concentrate with high levels of caffeine from coffee, tea or a square of dark chocolate, yet don't overdo.

Chew gum

This old-school behaviour can momentarily enhance awareness and perhaps also extend your interest at the end stages of longer tasks. Eating gum tissue is likewise related to reducing chronic stress and anxiety, one more useful element for emphasis.

Go outside

Studies have actually shown that individuals can focus much better after communing with nature or perhaps simply looking at images of nature, according to study studies. If it's simply a walk in the park-- can calm all the stimulations that get your spontaneous attention, subjective experience--

even. Nature allows your focused mind remainder and also refreshing.

Meditate and also be conscious

Numerous research studies show that practising meditation for 20mins a day boosts both concentration and also attention period. The easiest means to start meditating is to start noticing your breathing-- becoming "conscious" of it-- over the course of a minute or two. Next session, focus much more intently on your breathing for 5-10mins twice a day-- in the morning and before bed. When you get distracted, bring your consciousness back to your inhales and exhales.

Take control of your capability to focus

Do something regarding it now prior to it obtains worse if concentrating has ended up being a lot more difficult for you. Take control of your focusing setting by utilizing several of the suggestions over. You can also attempt the adhering to strategies that you may have discovered as a pupil. They truly assist:

1. Operate in "pieces:" Divide your work into parcels and take pleasure in a timeout between each chunk.

2. Relax: Remaining on the very same task or topic for as well lengthy exhaustions the mind, just as way too much workout lady wears down the body.

3. Set a goal: Establish an endpoint for your task and reward on your own when you reach it with a refreshing beverage, a social telephone call, or a stroll outside. For longer work, intend them out in phases and take little breaks in between each phase-- just enough time to remainder without damaging your energy.

Another approach to take when you can't focus is to listen to your brain and your body and take a remainder or switch to a various task briefly. If being able to concentrate really feels impossible for you, it's time to make some of these changes.

Addition:

3 uncommon ways to boost focus

1. PRACTICE FOCUSING WHEN YOU DON'T HAVE TO:: review in a noisy spot or drive without the radio on.

2. SHAKE YOUR TOES: this mindfulness technique brings you back to the present if your concentration drifts.

3. AIM HIGH: Perform tasks that need extreme emphasis, like finding out a language, to activate the centre basalis-- your mind's mechanism for developing brand-new neural pathways and enhancing existing ones, additionally called neuroplasticity.

THE IMPORTANCE OF BEING FOCUSED

Being focused means you are in control of your life, feel a lot more favourable and know what is necessary to you today and also keeping that you can determine where you wish to be in the future. Most of us will agree that being focused permits us to be much more effective, and it brings clearness to our decision-making procedure. However, in our fast-paced, chaotic life, it comes to be increasingly more challenging for us to remain focused.

What's the alternative to being concentrated? When we lose our emphasis, we do a whole lot of whatever and accomplish nothing, and we jump from one task to the following without ever before getting anything done, and our options are dictated by other people's priorities, a feeling of seriousness and also what seems to be the most convenient way out.

If we are focused, we have a clear objective in mind and are dedicated to attaining our goals and desires. Every decision we make is based on just how we can most progress in the direction of our goals and dreams and also being concentrated in today minute enables us to be immersed in one solitary activity up until it is finished without letting distractions discourage us.

There are endless advantages of being focused, but we locate our complying with TOP 10 to be the most crucial.

1 Focus Reduces Stress

Without emphasis, we can easily come to be overwhelmed, demotivated or annoyed, and also we try to do as well much in too little time. When we start to concentrate, we gain quality and also recognize what is most crucial, and with that, we can get away the sensations of being bewildered and significantly reduce our stress and anxiety degrees.

#2 Focus Makes Us Faster

When we find our focus and also place all our power, attention and also effort on one single job without letting anything or anyone sidetracks us, our mind absolutely zeros in on the job handy and we can complete it much faster than if we were attempting to do 2 or more jobs simultaneously. Bear in mind; our mind is even more effective than any computer system can be with its unlimited creative thinking and knowledge and also when we focus, all its remarkable power enters into this one task, enabling us to hit our objective on schedule, every time.

#3 Focus Increases Engagement

Most individuals aren't afraid to put in the hard work that is required to get points done, but the majority of us hesitate of failure, and when we don't recognize where we are going and how we can arrive, it is quite tough to be engaged in the task available. When we are focused, we obtain clearness on where we desire to go and also why we desire to obtain there and also with that we obtain excited concerning what we are doing and raise our involvement particularly when we start to see the development

#4 Focus Produces Higher Quality

Being focused methods that we offer all our attention to the job handy without letting interruptions interfere and also with that said, we do not just get our job done more quickly. However, we likewise eliminate the possibilities of mistakes.

Whatever we do will go to a higher quality which concentrated focus likewise enhances our creative thinking, which permits us to come up with new ideas that are related to the job we are servicing.

5 Focus Makes You Feel in Control

Focus implies that we have the ability to focus on our master plan and also are in control of everyday disturbances. Of course, that doesn't indicate that unpredicted things will not happen, yet with a laser-sharp focus, we are far more certain and also prepared to manage anything that life puts in our method. And sure, most of us experience uncertainty and instabilities every now and then, however with our goals and dreams constantly in the leading edge of our mind, it's much easier to conquer them and also locate a means to fix any kind of challenge or obstacle and have the capacity to come up with a backup strategy.

#6 Focus Increases Positivity

The structure for success is to have an objective, remain and also produce a strategy focused on it. Keeping that, we build self-confidence in what we know and a solid idea that we can attain anything we established our mind to, which creates a positive, positive mindset that further sustains our goals. Our psychological state drives our resolution and also allows us to achieve what we laid out to do, so it is detrimental to get our mind in a state of positivity through focus.

#7 Focus Builds Momentum

We've seen earlier that being concentrated makes us faster while generating higher quality job and also with this boosted effectiveness, we develop progress that is extremely encouraging and constructs energy so that we can also attain larger and much better things. Seeing progress motivates us to function harder since we can see that our efforts bring outcomes, and when the sphere begins rolling, there is no quitting us.

#8 Focus Boosts Creativity

Distractions lose a great deal of mental capacity however being focused ways that all our mental capacity is available to the task available and it comes to be a great deal less complicated ahead up with brand-new, innovative ideas. Whatever area you are in, whether you are a typical imaginative like an artist or musician or a unique imaginative like an entrepreneur or stay-at-home parent, we can all benefit from an additional boost to our innovative circulation, and a little focus goes a long means.

9 Focus Improves Joy

With all the various other advantages of being concentrated, it doesn't come as a surprise that a focused mind results in a happy mind. Having the capacity to centre ourselves and focus our attention on what is most important to us and bring about efficient behaviour permits us to take control of our life and also where and exactly how we concentrate our interest and power.

Focus permits us to choose what type of person we intend to be, and once we are running as our best self; we have the ability to live our best, happiest life.

#10 Focus Brings Clarity to What You Want and What You Don't Want

When we don't recognize what we want, we get caught up in desiring to take every chance that comes our way and also winds up wasting our time, power and focus on points that do not really issue. However, when we are focused, we have the power to identify what we desire out of life just like we figure out what we don't want and we are able to carry our energy and bring clearness to the instructions we intend to guide our life to.

We stay in a globe of consistent distractions from our cell phones to TV, net, radio, social media and the large populace living closer with each other than ever. This makes it very easy to obtain lugged away and attempt to complete a million and one points all at ones. However, this is nothing more than rubbish, because, in order to be efficient and effective in life, it is essential that we learn to concentrate on one purpose each time and persevere until its completion.

HOW FOCUS WORKS IN YOUR BRAIN

Even while your mind is focusing now as you read this article, you may not discover it. Still, a minimum of three various types of interest are generating your ability to concentrate and concentrate:

1. Selective attention to focus on one thing whilst neglecting others.

2. Separated interest, likewise understood as "interest switching," for handling and processing multiple resources of info at the exact same time. Separated interest is particularly vulnerable to modifications as you get older but both

cardiovascular workout and also method switching back and also forth in between tasks can help preserve focus.

3. Sustained attention for remaining focused on something for a long time. Your mind sorts and also route info so you can concentrate amidst all the distractions and input that pester you every day. Your brain directs focus capability by filtering essential info and relocating it up the ladder for deeper processing while reducing disturbances from unnecessary little bits and pieces-- a function recognized as an efficient option.

How disruptions break your focus

Even with its elegant processing filters, your mind can still lose its focus. Loud sounds and also blinking lights create lots of neural lights task which makes them zoom to the leading edge of your awareness, leaving behind whatever you had been concentrating on. That's useful on a field of battle or when you will crash your cars and truck, but not if you're trying to study for a test and also a neighbouring car alarm breaks your concentration.

To remain focused, your mind needs a "braking system" to prevent incorrect points from jumping back into your head. And the VLPFC still obstructs interruptions-but some brains are much better off using these brakes than others because the VLPFC is weak and uses a lot of energy.

The cost of being distracted

Despite the fact that interruptions are the number one variable that hinders focus, much of them are self-induced. Because we have too much info (TMI) generally coming with us all day, our brains can just get overwhelmed. TMI-- specifically at work-- weakens our effectiveness and dulls our emphasis.

They utilize up our restricted attention period and also avoid us from moving into much deeper   iStock_000015886014XSmallthought procedures when essential. Ping-ponging from topic to subject uses up power and also fuel-- your brain is powered by glucose-- so it's tougher to understand, choose, recall, memorize and control what you do.

Lack of focus tries every little thing in your life-- consisting of the enjoyable stuff. Lots of people are ashamed to admit that they can not concentrate enough time to read a paragraph, not to mention a whole publication. Quickly after they have actually checked out a sentence, they can not inform you anything regarding what it claimed.

If you can not concentrate well, your confidence wears down and insecurity constructs, and that can lead to impatience, depression, and stress and anxiety. You might snap at associates or family members, eventually abandoning things you wished to share or accomplish with others.

What exactly is distracting you?

Social media site, email, cell phones and also the net allow focus thieves. One research study showed that overeating in social media sites and online searching could be worse than shedding a night's rest, and even cigarette smoking cannabis. Men are twice as likely to be distracted by multielectronic connection.

Numerous major diversions are because of the reality that our minds tend to wander. Something referred to as ambient neural activity. This dreaminess is likely an outcome of the nervous system continually refining, reconfiguring, losing touch and after that reconnecting.

Once a diversion penetrates your emphasis-- an arriving e-mail or perhaps simply getting out of your chair-- it's difficult to stop yourself from checking out better because your emphasis has actually currently moved. Now, the distraction becomes your major emphasis and also the task you were dealing with fades to history.

Does getting older blur your focus? Yes — and no

In between ages 40 and also 60, the areas of the brain that reduce disturbances might slow down so you can locate it tougher to ignore distractions or unnecessary details. Adjustments to particular facets of perception, attention and memory-- the mind's "very early handling" locations-- will impact cognitive function down the line.

We're all various and so are our minds-- lots of older folks have sharp focus into their 70s and 80s. And others may have reduced concentration in particular areas but not others.

This variability results from a series of variables, some biological or emotional, with others a lot more pertaining to health and wellness, setting, and particularly lifestyle. A great deal of recent clinical studies looked at the results of way of living on brain function. As you could forecast, an active lifestyle helps keep your mind healthy, and cardio workout is particularly great for the mind.

Just because you are ageing doesn't imply you'll end up with fuzzy reasoning or inadequate emphasis, especially if you do something currently to assist you to remain sharp.

BRAIN GAMES FOR YOUNGSTERS TO ENHANCE CONCENTRATION

We might not realize it, but focusing is harder than it appears! Below is a terrific checklist of 12 mind ready youngsters that will certainly help enhance to concentrate and remember. It functions wonderful on both youngsters and adults alike!

Well, there are many video games that you can play to boost your degree of concentration. In this guide, we take you via the 12 finest brain games that you can start playing right away to enhance your concentration span.

1. Crossword Games

These games are amongst the most effective cognitive exercises as they test your mind to focus as you try to identify the responses.

Apart from aiding, you to boost your concentration, they likewise enable you to reduce the threat of mental deterioration.

2. Jigsaw Puzzles

The even more items there are, a lot more your brain has to work. Fixing jigsaw challenges every day can help you boost your concentration a great deal.

3. Chess

If you are searching for a video game that will certainly force you to think critically and logically after that, chess is what you require. Playing chess forces you to think about utilizing your entire mind (both sides).

This can help you considerably in improving your concentration. This game challenges you to be creative to fix troubles. So, you have to focus a great deal to do that well sufficient to win.

4. Sudoku

Solving this game trains your mind to absorb a number of methods and also pieces of details in a short period. As a result, playing sudoku forces your mind to concentrate so you can put all the numbers in order without any rep. By doing so, this game promotes your mind to believe fast and makes you better in tasks that need a great deal of concentration and reasoning.

5. Brain Teasers

These video games are great for testing the mind to focus for you to figure them out as they also consist of puzzles. By doing so, mind teasers aid you develop your brain muscle mass and boost your concentration levels.

6. Shopping Games

One more perfect method of improving your concentration degrees is trying to memorize a wish list. You need to utilize secure words to aid you to symbolize what is in fact on your wish list.

When you use them to represent the precise points on your checklist, it can make it very easy for you to bear in mind the points you require to purchase in the appropriate order without neglecting a thing.

Utilizing various other points to symbolize stuff on your buying listing forces you to concentrate, so you don't forget the real things you have on your listing.

7. Brain Yoga

Brain yoga exercise might appear basic but can challenge your mind concentration a lot. Exactly how this game works is you have to make a clenched fist with your left hand and then prolong your pinky finger. You require to make a fist with your right-hand man also only that you'll require to expand your thumb this moment.

Afterwards, you need to try alternating in that your right-hand man extends the pinky finger while the left expands the thumb. Currently, try doing it severally. Not so simple right? Playing brain yoga needs a great deal of coordination to do it appropriately.

Doing it a few times a day can help you improve your concentration substantially.

8. Lumosity

Lumosity is among the best video games that you can play to help you enhance your mental skills. Neuroscientists developed this application to assist people efficiently enhance their concentration levels and also assume faster. Utilizing this app for simply a session each day can assist you to increase your concentration degrees a great deal.

9. Tray Video game

To play this video game, place some random products on a tray then ask someone to hold it for you. When you provide down whatever you remember, reveal the tray and see if there is something you did miss out on.

10. Rebus Puzzle

This game is outstanding as it makes use of phrases with concealed significances, which after that requires you to focus on the words to figure out what they mean.

For example, an expression like" negative" can privately suggest dreadful. You'll require to take a while to think of the phrase repeatedly to solve the problem. You must focus hard. By doing so, this game allows you to boost your concentration degrees.

11. Suitcase Game

You have to play this game with a group of individuals. A single person needs to state that he/she has chosen an item to pack in a suitcase. The next gamer discusses a different item and additionally states what the previous individual chose.

You are automatically out of the game if you can't remember what the previous person stated or miss out on one product in the list.

12. Video Games

When you are still playing, there are video clip games that require you to multitask or respond to brand-new environments. These video games can be perfect for increasing your concentration as they require your brain to concentrate, so you do not miss out on any kind of information. For more youthful youngsters computer game need to be made use of at the discernment of the moms and dads.

There are many brain games that you can play to assist you to boost your concentration. Some of these video games can obtain repeated and end up being easy to address after playing for some time. When this occurs, guarantee you obtain an additional game, so you maintain testing your mind with various things.

CAN VIDEO GAMES IMPROVE ATTENTION AND FOCUS?

Researchers at the Universities of Rochester and also Wisconsin carried out an experiment on the results of technology use on interest and cognition. The initial is media multitasking. Media multitasking is specified as being able to use two or even more media innovations at the same time, such as looking at social media while both texting and viewing television.

Playing activity video games, on the other hand, is proven to improve focus. This research asked the inquiry: Does heavy gaming, which boosts attention, soften the negative results of media multitasking?

Individuals were asked to submit sets of questions regarding their media use and also their video game usage. These questionnaires were used to categorize individuals as light, tool or hefty multitaskers, based upon a number of media jobs carried out simultaneously. Video clip players were classified based on the number of hrs each week they played games.

As soon as the participants were categorized on both scales-- multitasking and gaming-- they were offered four jobs to finish that required numerous degrees of attention.

Surprisingly sufficient, the centre media multitaskers executed much better at finishing the tasks than the light and also heavy media multitaskers. But gamers evaluated surpassed the non-gamers whatsoever degrees. So, as an example, non-gamer, light media multitaskers executed worse than a gamer, light media multitaskers. This outcome brought about two basic conclusions.

1) Media multitasking negatively influenced the efficiency of the experiment jobs. Medium multi-tasking impacted attention the least, yet if pushed into heavy multitasking, the focus was extremely negatively affected.

2) Video gaming appeared to balance out a few of the negative results of multitasking on focus.

The surprise was that, as soon as multitasking was thought about hefty, pc gaming had little or no positive influence on interest.

Scientists used the very same media-usage and gaming sets of questions as previous researches. Researchers likewise used the very same attention jobs as previous scientists to gauge attentiveness and also cognition. These 2 factors reveal that these researchers were cautious about developing their research study to be suitable with previous studies of the exact same subject so the outcomes could be thought about an extension of the previous research.

This research is vital due to the fact that it suggests that playing video games can be helpful for boosting focus. It also functions as a cautionary tale. It shows up that hefty media multitasking contributes to a lack of interest and also, in extreme situations, video game use does not help offset that adverse impact. Use one electronic tool at once.

Moderation is best!